KIDS GET CODING

PROGRAMMING GAMES AND ANIMATION

Heather Lyons

Illustrations by Alex Westgate & Dan Crisp

Lerner Publications ◆ Minneapolis

Contents

Children will need access to the Internet for most of the activities in this book. Parents or teachers should supervise Internet use and discuss online safety with children.

Getting Started

Hi! I'm Data Duck! I am going to show you how to make your own computer game. In order to make a game, we need to design what it will look like. To make it work, we need to use computer code.

We will also look at how we can animate a character in a game. To animate means to bring to life—this means we will write code that makes the character move!

DATA DUCK

Computer code is a set of rules or instructions. These instructions tell the computer how our game works, what it looks like, and how it is played. The code we will be using is made of blocks. Each block has a different set of instructions in it. When we place these blocks in the right order, we can make our computer do all sorts of things!

There are lots of activities in the book for you to try out. There are also some online activities for you to practice. For the online activities, go to **www.blueshiftcoding.com/kidsgetcoding** and look for the activity with the page number from the book.

Games in All Shapes and Sizes!

Computer games are great fun! Have you ever played a computer game? Do you have a favorite one? Which computer do you play it on?

We can play computer games on all kinds of computers. A computer is anything that works with a computer "brain," or a microprocessor. Cell phones, tablets, and games consoles are all computers.

DATA DUCK

Gaming goggles are worn like glasses. They cover your eyes with a screen, showing the game you are playing. This makes you feel like you're really inside the game. Gaming goggles can even be used to control the game by picking up on the way your body is moving!

Let's Play!

Look at this living room. Can you pick out the items here that can be used to play computer games?
Can you think of other things you might use to play a computer game?

Turn to page 23 to see the answers.

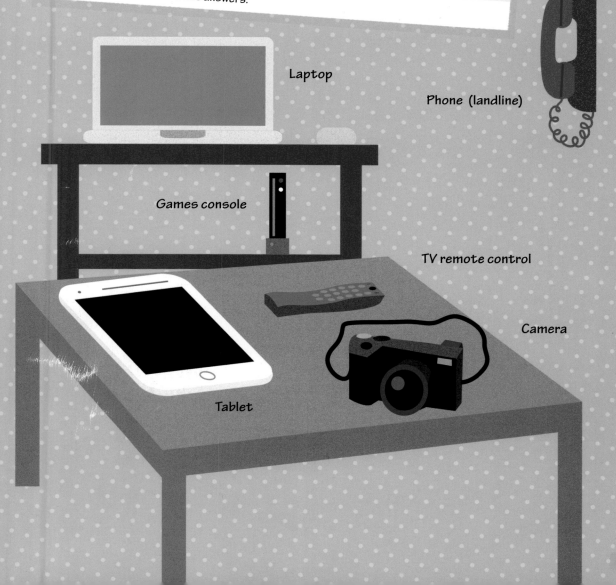

Laptop

Phone (landline)

Games console

TV remote control

Camera

Tablet

Story Time

Most games either tell a story or give you a challenge to complete, such as winning a race. Do you like games about sports such as football or tennis? Or do you prefer playing a character who goes on an adventure and maybe hunts for treasure?

Let's design our game to have a story. It will be about a character named Amy who has to get through a maze to find a treasure. To begin with, we need to think more about the story our game will tell, and what our maze, treasure, and character will look like.

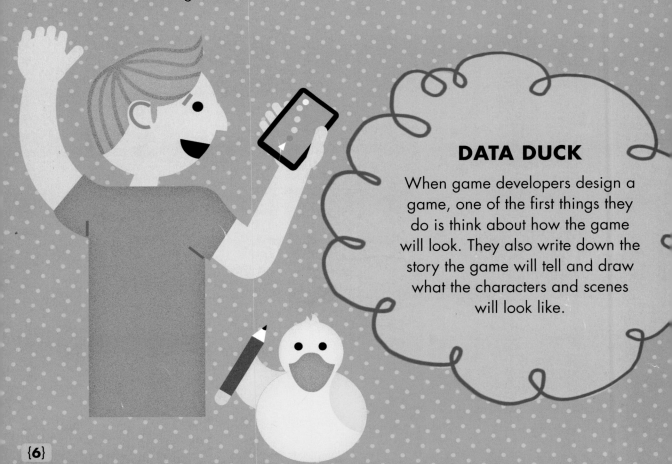

DATA DUCK

When game developers design a game, one of the first things they do is think about how the game will look. They also write down the story the game will tell and draw what the characters and scenes will look like.

Setting the Scene

Trace our maze on a piece of graph paper. Where should the treasure be, and what should it look like? Where will Amy start from at the beginning of the game? What should she look like?

Keep on Moving

Coding a game is a bit like making a story come to life. So let's think about what we would like our character, Amy, to do. For example, how does the person playing the game move Amy through our maze?

We will need Amy to move in four directions to get through the maze. The player will use the arrow keys on the computer keyboard to move Amy. So we need to write a code that tells the computer what to do each time an arrow is pressed.

Ready, Steady, Go!

Let's try to code an animation. Look carefully at the groups of coding blocks below. The first group is correct, but there is a word missing from each of the other three groups. Choose where each of these words needs to go to complete each instruction: down, up, left.

Turn to page 23 to see the answers.

DATA DUCK
Bringing a character to life and getting it to move across the screen is called animation. We can also animate words and objects. Anything that moves around our screen is animated.

```
When right arrow key is pressed

    Point in right direction

    Move 10 steps
```

```
When down arrow key is pressed

    Point in _____ direction

    Move 10 steps
```

```
When left arrow key is pressed

    Point in _____ direction

    Move 10 steps
```

```
When up arrow key is pressed

    Point in _____ direction

    Move 10 steps
```

Look Out!

In every good game, there are many characters and challenges to overcome. Villains are a great way to add a challenge for the character. Villains can take away points or lives, so the character needs to avoid them—if she can!

What does the villain in our game look like? Can you draw him or her? Think about what this villain can do—can the villain run very fast? This would make it hard for Amy to stay away. It would be a fun challenge!

DATA DUCK
We can animate our character to jump, run, and cheer using costumes.

Danger Ahead!

When we program how a character should look, we use the word *costume*. Our character, Amy, may hold up an arm when she finds something. This might be called Costume A. A character can have many costumes. There are a few examples below.

Costume A

Costume B

Costume C

We can program the computer to switch between two costumes again and again, with a short break between each switch:

When Amy is clicked

Repeat 10 times

Switch to Costume B

Pause for 1 second

Switch to Costume A

Pause for 1 second

Can you figure out what this code does? Look at the costumes on the left to help you.

Turn to page 23 to see the answers.

Treat Time

Now that we have a villain chasing our character, let's think about how we can reward our character. Maybe we can hide little treats around the maze. Every time our character eats a treat, she scores points!

Think about the kinds of treats you would like to add to your game. Maybe some candy? Or a tasty piece of fruit?

Design three treats and write down how many points each of them gives our character.

DATA DUCK
Sometimes we use "if statements" when we code. These tell the computer to carry out an action, but only after something else has happened. For example, *If* Amy eats a snack, *then* award two points.

Gobble, Gobble!

Once Amy has found a treat, we want her to eat it, receive points, and make a noise. We can program these activities using code. Look at the blocks of code below and put them in the right order.

If touching treat then

Play sound "That was tasty!"

Change score by +2

Show picture of treat half-eaten

Turn to page 23 to see the answers.

High Score!

We have thought about how Amy can collect points with treats and lose lives with villains. Now we need to write the code that helps our computer keep score for us!

How will our scoring system work? For example, our character may start with three lives and zero points.

• When a villain catches our character, she loses a life.

• When our character eats a treat, she gets 2 points.

• When Amy finds the treasure, she has completed the maze!

DATA DUCK
There are many different ways of scoring computer games. The great thing about coding our own game is that we can choose whichever scoring system we like best!

+1

Adding Up

Let's look at some of the code we need for our scoring system. Out of the two groups of coding blocks, pick the correct one in each group.

Turn to page 23 to see the answers.

```
If touching villain then

    Change lives by +2
```

```
If touching villain then

    Change lives by -2
```

```
If touching villain then

    Change lives by -1
```

```
If touching treat then

    Change score by +2
```

```
If touching treat then

    Change score by +20
```

```
If touching treat then

    Change score by -20
```

Level Up

Many games have levels. The higher the level, the more difficult most games become. In our game, moving to the next level may make the maze harder, or more villains could start chasing the character.

How do we change levels using code? When the character finds the treasure in level 1, we can send a message to the background image of our game. The message will change the background to a more difficult maze.

When I receive message "level up"

Switch background to level 2 maze

Level 2

Now that we have moved on to level 2, we need to think about the new background of our game. What will the new, harder maze look like? Using graph paper, design the next maze for your game.

DATA DUCK
Some games have lots of levels—up to 100 or more! But we have to be careful not to put in too many levels or no one will ever finish the game!

Let's Celebrate!

Now that we have designed the levels of the game, we need to think about how and when it ends. The end of a game means that the player has won, so we need to make sure getting there is a challenge!

Let's say that our game has ten levels, and at the end, the player needs to find one final treasure to win the game. Now we need to think about how we will celebrate the player's success. Let's tell them how well they've done!

Victory Dance

At the end of our game, the computer will show the player's final score. Then, we would like Amy to do a victory dance. Look at the costumes below. What instructions would you give the computer to have Amy do your victory dance?

DATA DUCK
Many games finish with animation. Sometimes it's just the main character. Other times the entire cast of the game is celebrating together—even the villains!

Costume A:
Right arm stretched up

Costume C:
Both arms stretched up

Costume B:
Left arm stretched up

Costume D:
Jumping up

The Final Test

As with all computer code, we need to make sure ours works properly by testing it. So we need to look through our code carefully to make sure there aren't any bugs.

Programmers can check their work by sending their game to lots of different players. The players all try out the game and let the programmer know if they find mistakes. Then the programmers look at the code to find out where the problem is and to decide how to fix it.

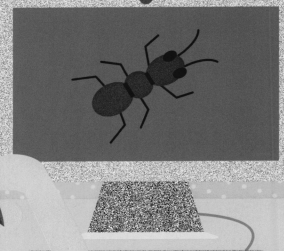

DATA DUCK

Bugs are mistakes in coding. They can mean a game can't be played properly. There are lots of different kinds of bugs. Sometimes coding blocks are in the wrong order, and sometimes they're missing altogether.

Debug It!

Amy is supposed to lose a life every time she touches a villain. Can you figure out why she isn't by looking at the coding blocks?

Turn to page 23 to see the answers.

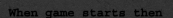

When game starts then

Set lives to 3

Forever

If touching treat then

Change lives by -1

Extension Activities

Go to **blueshiftcoding.com/kidsgetcoding** to make your own maze game and to practice

- animating characters
- creating scoring systems
- debugging your games

Words to Remember

animate   to bring something on screen to life by making it move

bug   an error in a computer program

code   the arrangement of instructions in a computer program

costume   the appearance of a character in a computer game

debug   to find and remove bugs or errors in a computer program

programmer a person who builds computer programs

Activity Answers

Page 5
Items that can be used to play computer games:

laptop

tablet

games console

Other devices include: cell phone, desktop computer

Page 9

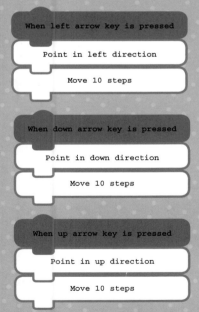

```
When left arrow key is pressed
    Point in left direction
        Move 10 steps
```

```
When down arrow key is pressed
    Point in down direction
        Move 10 steps
```

```
When up arrow key is pressed
    Point in up direction
        Move 10 steps
```

Page 11
This code will change between Amy's two poses (Costume A and Costume B) 10 times. There will be a one-second pause between each pose. Because we are moving between poses quite quickly, it will look like Amy is moving!

Page 13

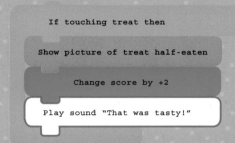

```
If touching treat then
    Show picture of treat half-eaten
        Change score by +2
Play sound "That was tasty!"
```

We could put "Play sound 'That was tasty!'" before "Change score by +2," but that would mean the sound would have to finish playing before the score changed. When we code, we have to pay very close attention to the order we put things in!

Page 15

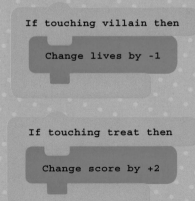

```
If touching villain then
    Change lives by -1
```

```
If touching treat then
    Change score by +2
```

Page 21
The code says that Amy loses a life every time she touches a treat!

Index

animate, 3, 9–10, 19

bug, 20–21

code, 3, 8–9, 11–16, 20–21

computer, 3–5, 8, 11–12, 14, 19–20

level, 16–18

programmer, 20

score, 12, 14, 19

villain, 10, 12, 14, 16, 19, 21

First American edition published in 2018 by Lerner Publishing Group, Inc.
First published in Great Britain in 2017 by Wayland, an imprint of Hachette Children's Group
Copyright © Hodder & Stoughton, 2017
Text copyright © Heather Lyons

All US rights reserved. No part of this book may be reproduced, stored in a retrieval system, or transmitted in any form or by any means—electronic, mechanical, photocopying, recording, or otherwise—without the prior written permission of Lerner Publishing Group, Inc., except for the inclusion of brief quotations in an acknowledged review.

Lerner Publications Company
A division of Lerner Publishing Group, Inc.
241 First Avenue North
Minneapolis, MN 55401 USA

For reading levels and more information, look up this title at www.lernerbooks.com.

Main body text set in Futura Std. Book 12/16. Typeface provided by Adobe Systems.

Library of Congress Cataloging-in-Publication Data
Names: Lyons, Heather (Heather K.), author. | Westgate, Alex, illustrator. | Crisp, Dan, illustrator. | Lyons, Heather (Heather K.). Kids get coding.
Title: Programming games and animation / Heather Lyons ; illustrated by Alex Westgate and Dan Crisp.
Description: Minneapolis, MN : Lerner Publications, [2017] | Series: Kids get coding | Audience: Ages 6-10. | Audience: K to grade 3. | Includes index.
Identifiers: LCCN 2016050902 (print) | LCCN 2016052677 (ebook) | ISBN 9781512439410 (lb : alk. paper) | ISBN 9781512455854 (pb : alk. paper) | ISBN 9781512450507 (eb pdf)
Subjects: LCSH: Computer games—Programming—Juvenile literature. | Computer animation—Programming—Juvenile literature.
Classification: LCC QA76.6 .L885625 2017 (print) | LCC QA76.6 (ebook) | DDC 005.1—dc23

LC record available at https://lccn.loc.gov/2016050902

Printed in China

The website addresses (URLs) included in this book were valid at the time of going to press.
However, it is possible that contents or addresses may have changed since the publication of this book.
No responsibility for any such changes can be accepted by either the author or the Publisher.